SCHOLASTIC

Pocket Chart Games

READING

by Angie Kutzer

New York · Toronto · London · Auckland · Sydney
Mexico City · New Delhi · Hong Kong · Buenos Aires

Teaching *Resources*

To my wonderful parents, David and Barbara,
Thanks for believing in me, even when I didn't believe in myself.
Your support and taxi service are greatly appreciated!

"For nothing is impossible with God."
—Luke 1:37 (NLT)

Edited by Immacula Rhodes
Cover design by Scott Davis
Interior design by Sydney Wright
ISBN 978-0-545-28075-4

Copyright © 2013 by Angie Kutzer.
Illustrations © 2013 by Scholastic Inc.
All rights reserved. Published by Scholastic Inc.
Printed in the U.S.A.

1 2 3 4 5 6 7 8 9 10   40   20 19 18 17 16 15 14 13

⁎ Contents ⁎

Introduction

Want to be sure that your students are getting effective practice in essential reading skills? *Pocket Chart Games: Reading* offers 15 engaging games that target the skills every child needs to master.

Research shows that a strong foundation in phonics, automatic recognition of spelling patterns, rhyming words, and sight words, and knowing and using vocabulary-related reading strategies are important components in building reading comprehension and fluency. The games in this book provide children of all learning styles with a motivating, fun way to practice and build skills while helping them meet important language arts standards. (See "Connections to the Common Core State Standards," page 6, for more.)

Everything you need is here and ready to use. The games are easy to prepare and can be set up in a snap—just pop the cards into a pocket chart and you're ready to go! In no time, children will be playing games such as "Letter Line-Up" to sequence letters, "Spidery Endings!" to create words by adding final consonants, "Blends Picnic" to identify beginning consonant blends, "Out of Sight!" to practice reading sight words, and many more. You can use the games with the whole class, small groups, or student pairs. And they're perfect for learning center activities!

What's Inside

The pocket-chart games in this book include the following:

* a list of materials needed to prepare and use the game
* preparation and setup directions
* a title card and activity cards
* step-by-step game directions
* an answer key, or suggestions for making the game self-checking
* ideas to introduce the targeted concept
* a list of helpful tips
* extension activities

Some games also include a practice page that provides additional reinforcement.

Preparing and Using the Pocket Chart Games

Most everything you need for the games is in this book, although some might require readily available materials such as paper clips, brass fasteners, markers, and masking tape. In addition to the listed materials, you'll need a standard-size pocket chart with clear pockets. To prepare and set up each game, simply follow the directions in Getting Ready.

Before children play the games independently, conduct mini-lessons to introduce the reading concept used in each game. Then play the game with children a few times to demonstrate how to play. Check that they understand the directions and game rules. After children become familiar with the game, you can use it as a learning center activity.

Following are useful tips to help you get the most from the games:

* To make the game pieces sturdy and more durable, copy them onto tagboard.

* Use crayons or markers to color the game components.

* Laminate the game pieces for durability.

* Store the components of each game in a large clasp envelope or gallon-size self-sealing plastic bag. Use a copy of the game title card as a label.

* Hang the pocket chart on a chart stand, bulletin board, or hooks mounted on a wall. After setting up the "path" games (such as "Blends Picnic"), you might lay the pocket chart on a flat surface so children can use it like a tabletop game board.

* Consider using the game or game components as part of your informal assessments. You can do this in a variety of ways, such as observing children as they play and noting their responses, or working with children in small groups or individually to evaluate their skills.

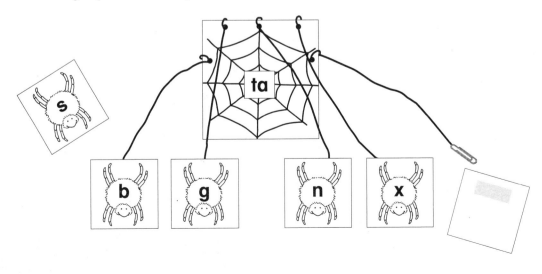

Connections to the Common Core State Standards

The Common Core State Standards Initiative (CCSSI) has outlined learning expectations in English Language Arts for students at different grade levels. The activities in this book align with the following standards for students in grades K–2. For more information, visit the CCSSI website at **www.corestandards.org**.

Reading Standards: Foundational Skills

Print Concepts
* Demonstrate understanding of the organization and basic features of print.
RF.K.1a, RF.K.1b, RF.K.1d

Phonological Awareness
* Demonstrate understanding of spoken words, syllables, and sounds (phonemes).
RF.K.2a, RF.K.2b, RF.K.2c, RF.K.2d, RF.K.2e
RF1.2a, RF1.2b, RF1.2c, RF1.2d

Phonics and Word Recognition
* Know and apply grade-level phonics and word analysis skills in decoding words.
RF.K.3a, RF.K.3b, RF.K.3c
RF.1.3a, RF.1.3b, RF.1.3c, RF.1.3d, RF.1.3e, RF.1.3g
RF.2.3a, RF.2.3b, RF.2.3c, RF.2.3f

Fluency
* Read emergent-reader texts with purpose and understanding.
RF.K.4

* Read with sufficient accuracy and fluency to support comprehension.
RF.1.4a, RF.1.4c
RF.2.4a, RF.2.4c

Answer Key: Practice Pages

page 17, Going for the Goal!
1. h
2. C
3. M
4. g
5. l
6. R

page 26, Starter Sounds
1. b
2. m
3. c
4. p
5. w
6. h
7. v
8. l
9. t

page 37, Vowel Swimmers
Children should color the fish with these words yellow: *clock, dog, flag, sled, wig,* and *sun.*
Children should color the fish with these words red: *cape, flute, note, seed, slide,* and *soap.*

page 57, Syllables at the Seashore
1. 2
2. 3
3. 1
4. 1
5. 2
6. 3
7. 2
8. 1
9. 2

Special Delivery Symbol Sort

Children distinguish letters from numbers and shapes in this postal-theme relay.

Players: 3 teams

Materials

- title card (page 8)
- game directions (page 9)
- category mailboxes (pages 8 and 12)
- envelope cards (pages 9, 10, and 11)
- answer key (page 12)
- pocket chart
- paper box lid (for letter tray)
- masking tape

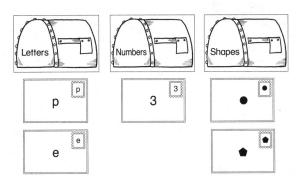

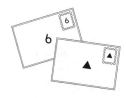

Getting Ready

Copy the title card, game directions, category mailboxes, envelope cards, and answer key. Cut out all of the game components. Place the title card in the top pocket of the pocket chart and spread out the mailboxes in the next pocket. Set the paper box lid upside down—to represent a letter tray—on the floor below the chart. (You might use pieces of rolled tape on the bottom of the tray to keep it from slipping around during play.) Spread the envelope cards facedown in the tray. Then tape a long start line on the floor, parallel to the chart and approximately 10–12 feet from it. Place the directions faceup and the answer key facedown in a pocket at the bottom of the chart. (Or use a clothespin to clip the answers to the side of the chart.)

Introducing the Game

Show children each game card. Explain that they should stand up if the card is labeled with a letter. Otherwise, they should remain seated. After children respond, invite a volunteer to identify the letter, number, or shape on the card. Next, display the mailboxes and read each label. Then pass out the cards, and invite children to place them with the corresponding mailbox. Decide with the class whether each card is placed with the correct mailbox. If incorrect, move the card to the correct mailbox. Finally, form three teams (six children per team) to play the game.

Extending the Game

- Tour the school with children to find examples of the alphabet, numbers, and shapes. You might take photos of the examples, print them in the size of the game envelopes, and cut out. Use the photos to make additional game cards.

- Invite children to create more game cards by cutting out examples of shapes, numbers, and letters from magazines.

- Place the pocket chart game in a center. Include a timer and challenge children to "deliver" the cards to the corresponding mailboxes within a given time.

HeLPFuL TiPS

- For younger children, add examples of the category to each mailbox for use as a reference. For instance, write a few letters on the "Letters" mailbox.

- Store the game cards in a miniature mailbox (available at craft stores).

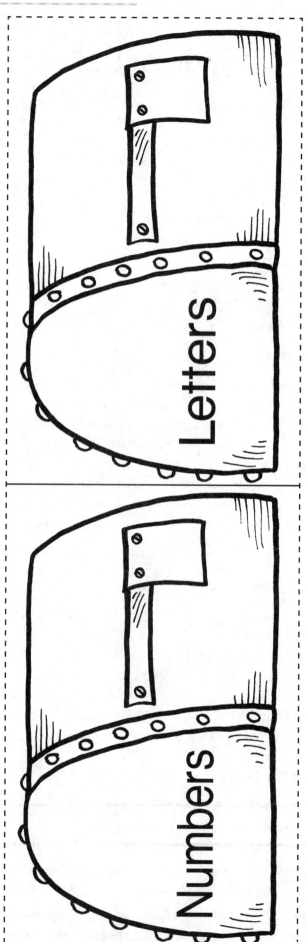

◇○□△◇○□△◇○□△ (Players: 3 teams) ◇○□△◇○□△◇○□△

Special Delivery Symbol Sort
Directions for Play

1 Each team chooses a mailbox. Team members line up at the Start line in front of their mailbox.

2 A player sounds a signal to start the game. The first player on each team walks quickly to the tray of cards.

3 The player looks for a card that matches his or her team's mailbox. When a card is found, the player puts it in a pocket below the mailbox.

4 The player goes back to Start and tags the next player on his or her team. That player walks quickly to the tray and repeats step 3.

5 Keep playing until one team matches six cards to its mailbox. That team then checks its answers. If correct, that team wins the game.

Pocket Chart Games: Reading © 2013 by Angie Kutzer, Scholastic Teaching Resources

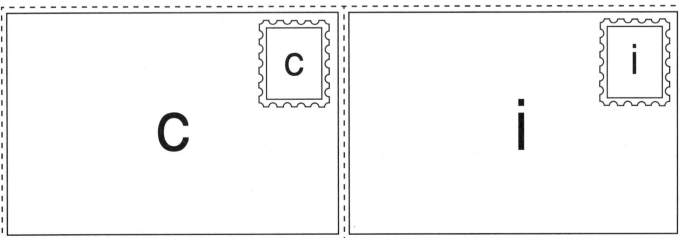

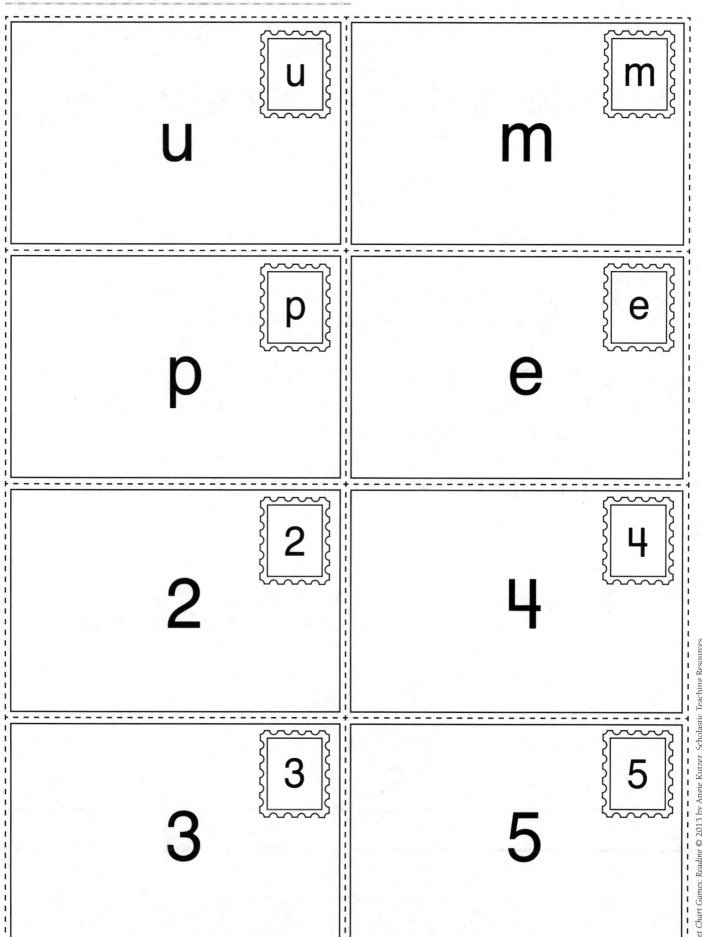

Pocket Chart Games: Reading © 2013 by Angie Kutzer, Scholastic Teaching Resources

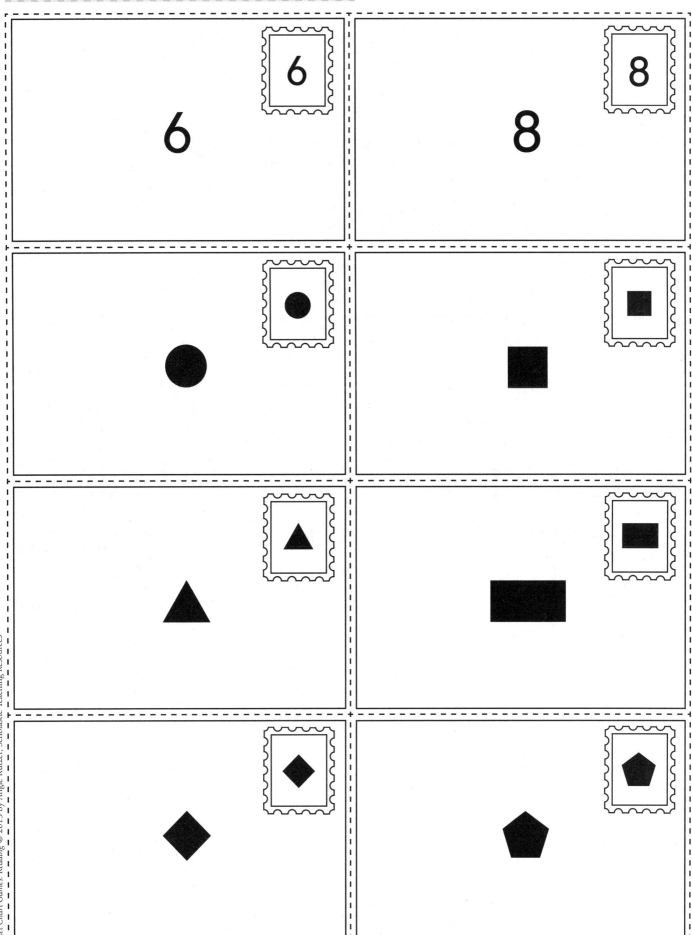

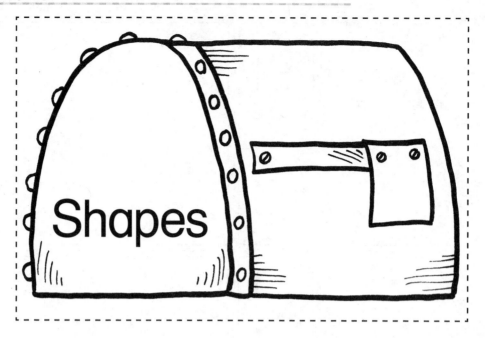

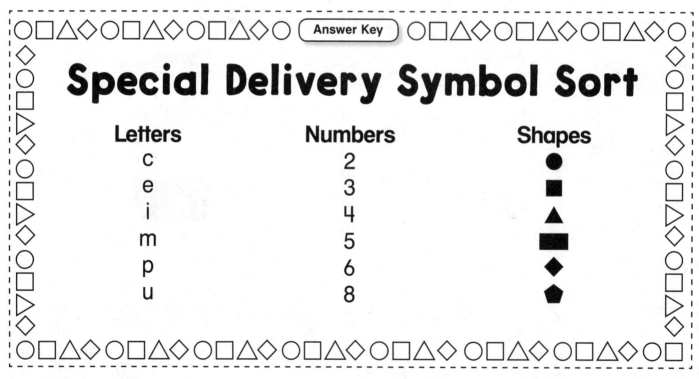

Answer Key

Special Delivery Symbol Sort

Letters	Numbers	Shapes
c	2	●
e	3	■
i	4	▲
m	5	▬
p	6	◆
u	8	⬟

Pocket Chart Games: Reading © 2013 by Angie Kutzer, Scholastic Teaching Resources

Alphabet SCORE!

Children score goals by identifying uppercase and lowercase letters.

Players: 2

Materials

- title card (page 14)
- game directions (page 15)
- soccer goals (page 14)
- soccer balls (page 16)
- answer key (page 15)
- 10 two-inch squares of green construction paper
- pocket chart
- practice page (page 17)

    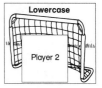

Getting Ready

Copy the title card, game directions, soccer goals, soccer balls, and answer key. Cut out all of the game components. Place the title card in the top pocket of the pocket chart. Put the goals in the far right side of the next two pockets. Line up five green squares to the left of each goal leaving some space between each one. Then shuffle the soccer balls and spread them out facedown in the chart below the goals. Place the directions faceup and the answer key facedown in the bottom pocket. (Or use a clothespin to clip the answers to the side of the chart.)

Introducing the Game

Place the soccer balls in a paper bag. Have children take turns drawing a ball from the bag, naming the letter, and telling whether it is an uppercase or lowercase letter. Then distribute the balls to children. (Or use uppercase and lowercase letter cards.) Explain that on a signal, children will group themselves by the type of letter on their cards: uppercase or lowercase. Afterward, review the letter cards with the class and have children correct their groupings, if needed. Finally, invite two children at a time to play the game.

Extending the Game

- For additional reinforcement, have children complete the practice page.
- Place the goals and soccer balls in a center. Invite children to sort the uppercase and lowercase letters. Or, have them match each lowercase letter to its corresponding uppercase letter.

HELPFUL TIPS

- If desired, have children play the game in two teams with three players each.
- Display an alphabet chart nearby for children to use as a reference.
- To give children practice with other letters, mask the letters on a copy of the soccer balls, label each pair with a different letter, and cut out.

13

Uppercase & Lowercase Letters

Alphabet SCORE!

Lowercase

Player 2

Uppercase

Player 1

Pocket Chart Games: Reading © 2013 by Angie Kutzer, Scholastic Teaching Resources

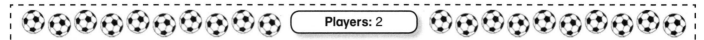

Players: 2

Alphabet SCORE!

Directions for Play

1 Each player chooses a soccer goal. Player 1 goes first.

2 Take a soccer ball and name the letter. Is it uppercase or lowercase?
- If the letter goes with your goal, put the ball on the first square on the left.
- If not, put the card back. Your turn ends.

3 Player 2 repeats step 2 on his or her turn.

4 Keep taking turns. Place your soccer balls from left to right. Put your last soccer ball on your goal.

5 The first player to reach his or her goal calls out "SCORE!" That player then checks his or her answers. If correct, the player wins the game.

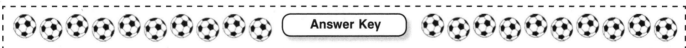

Answer Key

Alphabet SCORE!

Uppercase Letters		Lowercase Letters	
A	N	a	n
E	T	e	t
K	V	k	v

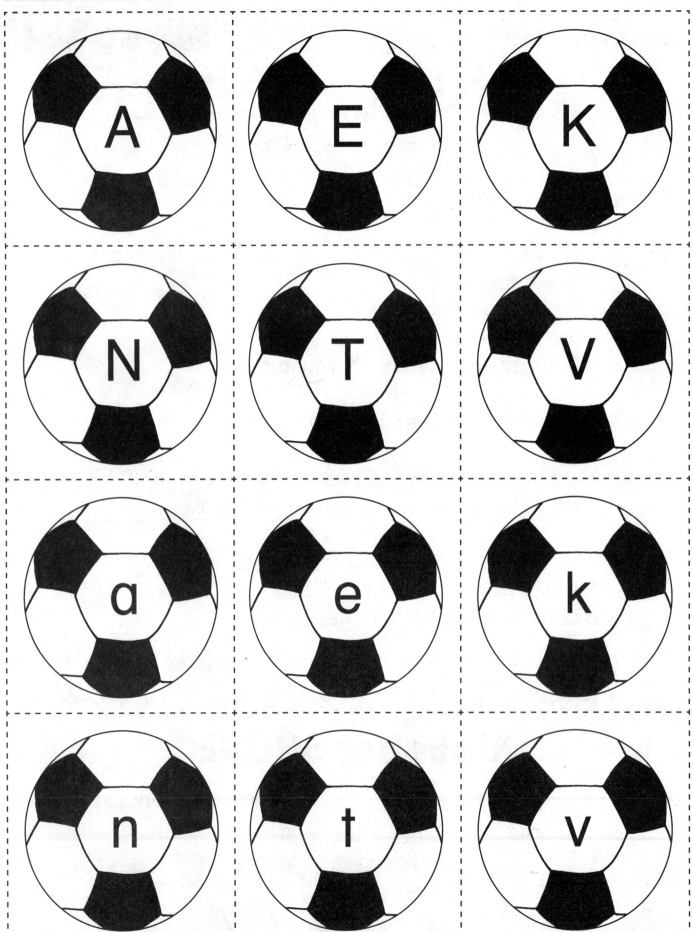

Pocket Chart Games: Reading © 2013 by Angie Kutzer, Scholastic Teaching Resources

Name _____ Date _____

Going for the Goal!

Cut out each ball.
Glue it to the goal with the matching letter.

1.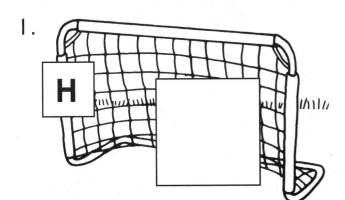

2.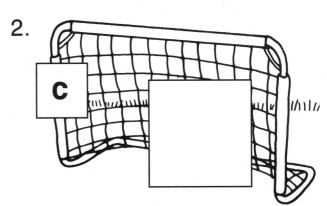

3.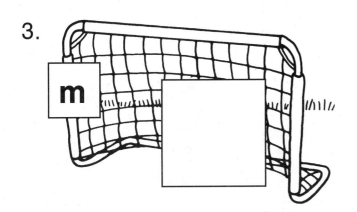

4.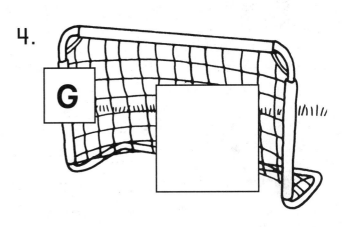

5.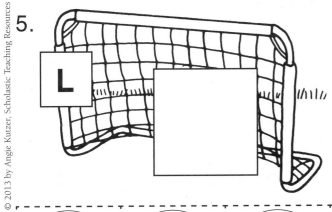

6.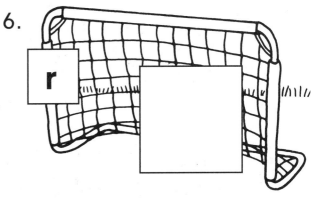

Letter Line-Up

Children compete to put a series of letters in alphabetical order in the shortest amount of time.

Players: 2

Materials

- title card (page 19)
- game directions (page 20)
- game cards (pages 19 and 20)
- pocket chart
- marker
- alphabet chart
- stopwatch (to keep time)

Getting Ready

Copy the title card, game directions, and game cards. Make two additional copies of each set of game cards. Color and cut out all of the game components. (You should have a total of 18 game cards: nine cards for each set of cards.) Write a series of consecutive letters on each set of cards, such as *E, F, G, H, I, J, K, L,* and *M*. Label the cards with either all uppercase or all lowercase letters, using a different series of letters for each set. Place the title card in the top pocket of the pocket chart. Then shuffle each set of letter cards. Insert one stack of cards on the left side of a middle pocket and the other stack on the right side. Finally, place the directions faceup in the bottom pocket and post an alphabet chart nearby for reference.

Introducing the Game

Sing the alphabet song with children several times. Each time, pause at a different place in the song and invite volunteers to tell which letter comes next. Have children refer to an alphabet chart, if needed. Then, using a set of game cards, work with children to put the letters in alphabetical order. Explain that in the game, they will sequence the letters as quickly as they can. Demonstrate timing a volunteer by showing children how to give a signal and start the stopwatch, then stop it when the volunteer completes the task. Also, show them how to read the time on the stopwatch and reset it for the next round. Finally, invite two children at a time to play the game.

Extending the Game

- Display a series of letters, then remove two or three letters from the line-up. Challenge children to identify the missing letters.

- For practice in ordering letters at random, call out a letter and have children name the next three letters.

- Program the game cards with short two- and three-letter words for children to alphabetize.

HeLPFUL TiPS

* You might prepare a mix of lowercase and uppercase letters when labeling the letter cards for older children.

* Copy additional sets of the game cards on different colors of paper and use them to make more letter sets so that more children can play the game.

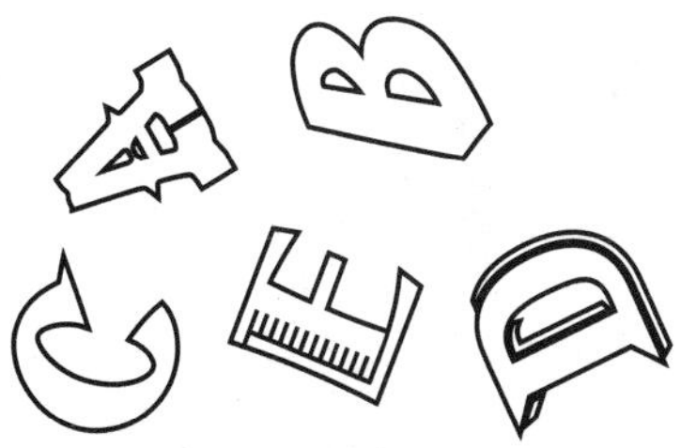

Letter Line-Up

Alphabetical Order

Pocket Chart Games: Reading © 2013 by Angie Kutzer, Scholastic Teaching Resources

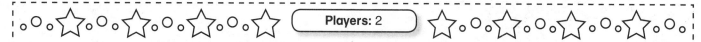

Players: 2

Letter Line-Up
Directions for Play

1 Choose a set of letter cards. Keep the cards stacked facedown.

2 Your partner says "Go!" and starts the timer.
At that time, turn your cards over. Put the letters in
alphabetical order. Line them up in a pocket.

3 When you finish, your partner stops the timer. How much time
did you take? Check your answers on the alphabet chart.
- If correct, your time stands.
- If not, try again. Your partner keeps time from where you
  stopped. Keep trying until you put all of the letters in the
  correct order.

4 Switch roles with your partner and repeat steps 1, 2, and 3.
Which player had the shortest time? That player wins the round.

5 Switch letter cards and play another round.

Sounds Dance-Around

Children identify beginning consonant sounds as they dance around the pocket chart to music.

Players: 2 teams

Materials

* title card (page 22)
* game directions (page 23)
* picture cards (pages 22, 23, 24, and 25)
* answer key (page 25)
* construction paper in various colors
* marker
* masking tape
* pocket chart and stand
* music player and lively music
* practice page (page 26)

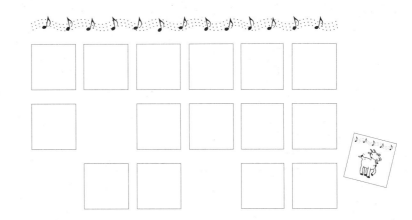

Getting Ready

Copy the title card, game directions, picture cards, and answer key. Cut out all of the game components. Place the title card at the top of the pocket chart. Then shuffle the picture cards and insert them facedown in the chart below the title. Place the directions faceup and the answer key facedown in the bottom pocket. Hang the pocket chart on a stand and place it in an open area. Use masking tape to make a large X on one sheet of construction paper. Tape that sheet on the floor directly in front of the chart. Then use additional sheets of construction paper to form a circular path around the chart (each sheet represents a stone). Use as many sheets as players for the game, and tape each one in place on the floor. Finally, set up chairs on opposite sides of the room and label each side with "Team 1" or "Team 2."

Introducing the Game

Display the picture cards one at a time. Have children name the picture and its beginning sound. Then write the word on the chalkboard and circle the beginning letter. Invite children to name other words that begin with the same letter. Next, tell children that the paper path around the pocket chart represents a stone path. Explain that they will move around the path to music, then "freeze" on the nearest stone when the music stops. If the nearest stone is already occupied, children should go to another stone. Finally, divide the class into two teams (Team 1 and Team 2) and point out where each team will sit as its members leave the game. At the start of the game, have each child stand between two members of the other team.

Extending the Game

* For additional reinforcement, have children complete the practice page.
* Place the picture cards in a learning center with a set of consonant alphabet cards. Have children match each picture to the letter for its beginning sound.

HeLPFuL TiPS

* Laminate the construction-paper "stones" for durability.
* In advance, establish guidelines for the kinds of dance and rhythmic movements children may perform.
* To warm up for the game, have children move around the path to a selection of lively music. Periodically stop the music, then direct children to step onto the nearest stone and "freeze."

Initial Consonants

Sounds Dance-Around

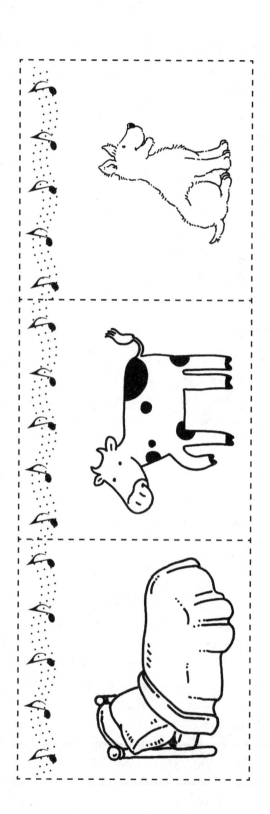

Pocket Chart Games: Reading © 2013 by Angie Kutzer, Scholastic Teaching Resources

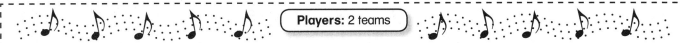

Players: 2 teams

Sounds Dance-Around
Directions for Play

1 Stand on a "stone" on the path.

2 When the music starts, dance around the path.
When it stops, move to the nearest stone and freeze.

3 If you stopped on the X, pick a card from the chart.
Name the picture. What letter does it begin with?

4 Check your answer.
• If correct, keep the card and sit in your team's area.
• If not, put the card back.

5 Continue until every player on one of the teams is seated.
That team wins the game.

Pocket Chart Games: Reading © 2013 by Angie Kutzer, Scholastic Teaching Resources

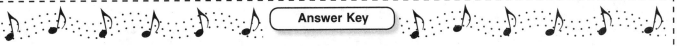

Answer Key

Sounds Dance-Around

bed	**j**et	**s**un
cow	**l**amp	**t**en
dog	**m**op	**v**an
five	**p**ig	**w**eb
goat	**q**uilt	**y**awn
hat	**r**ug	**z**ip

Starter Sounds

Name each picture.
Listen to the sound it begins with.
Circle the letter for that sound.

t   (d)   j

1.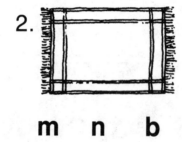

d   b   p

2.

m   n   b

3.

t   q   c

4.

m   b   p

5.

w   v   l

6.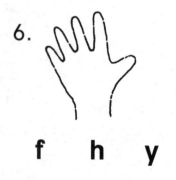

f   h   y

7.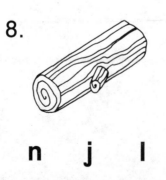

b   w   v

8.

n   j   l

9.

t   d   j

26

Spidery Endings

Children add consonant endings on spiders to letter pairs on webs to create CVC words.

Players: 2–4 players

Materials

- title card (page 28)
- game directions (page 29)
- spiders (pages 28, 29, and 30)
- webs (page 31)
- answer key (page 30)
- 20 six-inch lengths of kite string
- 20 metal paper clips
- self-adhesive magnet tape
- pocket chart

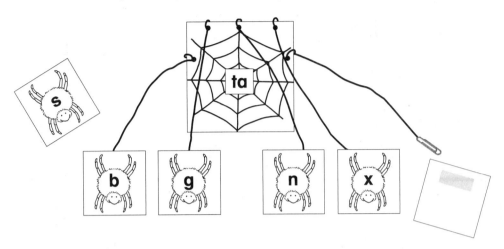

Getting Ready

Copy the title card, game directions, spiders, webs, and answer key. Make an additional copy of the spider cards on page 28. Cut out all of the game components. (You should have 22 spider cards.) Punch five small holes in each web where indicated. Tie one end of a length of string to each hole, then tie the other end to a paper clip. Place the title card in the top pocket of the pocket chart. Insert two webs on opposite sides of the next pocket and the other two webs several pockets below the first two. Check that the strings and paper clips hang loose in front of the webs. (Each string represents a spider dragline.) Affix a short strip of magnet tape to the back of each spider. Then shuffle the spiders and insert them facedown in the lower pockets of the chart. Place the directions faceup and the answer key facedown in the bottom pocket. (Or use clothespins to clip them to the side of the chart.)

Introducing the Game

Display the "bu" web and a spider for each letter in a pocket chart. Explain that children can make new words with the letters on the web and spiders. Demonstrate by placing the "g" spider to the right of the web and reading the resulting word, *bug*. Then attach a paper clip at the end of one of the draglines to the back of the spider. Tuck the spider into the pocket below the web. Continue making words until each dragline is attached to a spider. Then repeat for each of the remaining webs. Finally, invite 2–4 children to play the game.

Extending the Game

- Use the spider cards to reinforce letter sounds. Simply display one card per letter. Then say a word that ends in one of the letter sounds, such as *pot*, and have children identify that letter (t).

- Create additional webs and spiders that can be used to make other CVC words.

> ### HELPFUL TIPS
>
> * Use craft glue to help secure the paper clips to the strings. Do the same for the magnet strips on the back of the spider cards.
>
> * Remind children that not all letters on the spiders will make a word with the letter pair on a web. For example, *bu* and *p* do not make a word (*bup*).

Final Consonants

Spidery Endings

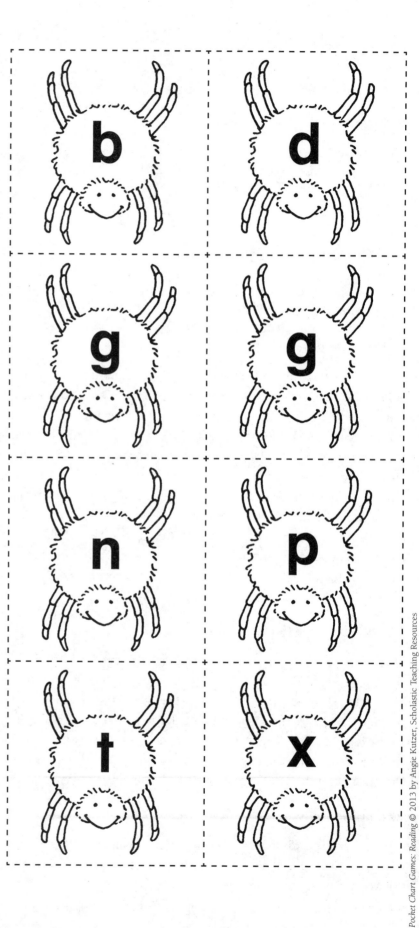

Pocket Chart Games: Reading © 2013 by Angie Kutzer, Scholastic Teaching Resources

Players: 2–4

Spidery Endings
Directions for Play

1 Each player chooses a spider web.

2 Take out a spider and name the letter.

3 Can you use that letter with the letters on your web to make a word? If so, name the word.

4 Check your answer.
- If correct, put the spider on a dragline. Then put it in the pocket below the web.
- If not, put the spider back.

5 Keep taking turns. The first player to match five spiders to his or web wins the game.

Pocket Chart Games: Reading © 2013 by Angie Kutzer, Scholastic Teaching Resources

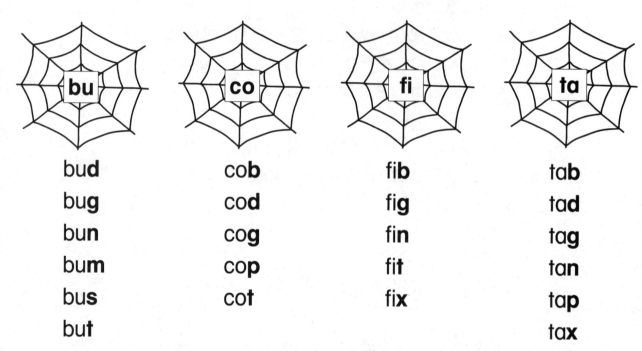

Answer Key

Spidery Endings

bud	cob	fib	tab
bug	cod	fig	tad
bun	cog	fin	tag
bum	cop	fit	tan
bus	cot	fix	tap
but			tax

Pocket Chart Games: Reading © 2013 by Angie Kutzer, Scholastic Teaching Resources

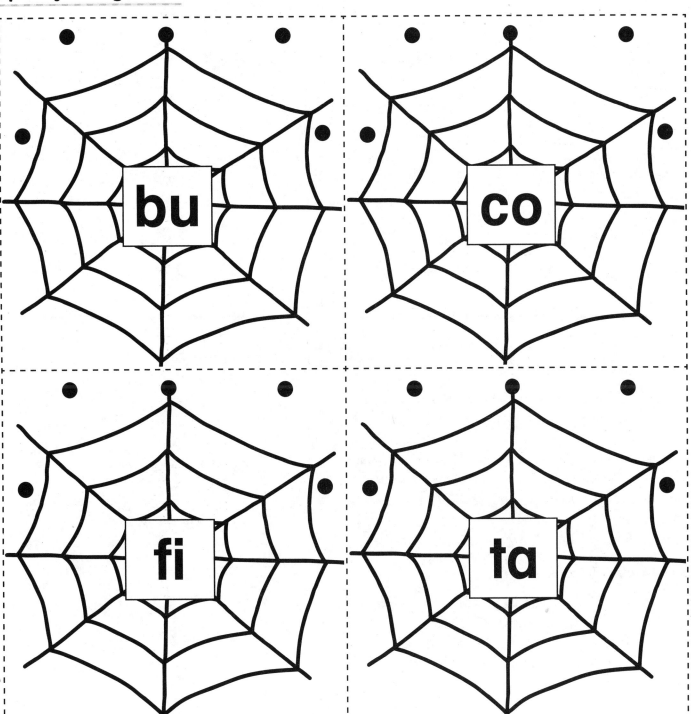

Fishing for Vowels

Children "catch" fish to practice identifying short and long vowel sounds.

Players: 2 or more

Materials

- title card (page 33)
- game directions (page 34)
- fish (pages 33, 34, 35, and 36)
- 21 large metal paper clips
- yardstick (or wooden dowel)
- three-foot length of yarn
- donut magnet
- pocket chart
- practice page (page 37)

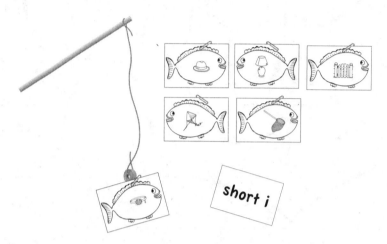

Getting Ready

Copy the title card, game directions, and fish. Color and cut out all of the game components. On the back of each fish, write the vowel sound for the picture on the front. Attach a paper clip to the top of each fish. Then place the title card in the top pocket of the pocket chart and the fish faceup in the pockets below the title. (Make sure the paper clips extend beyond the plastic pockets.) To make a fishing rod, tie one end of the length of yarn to the yardstick (or dowel) and the other end to the magnet.

Introducing the Game

Show children each fish and name the picture on it. Invite a volunteer to identify the vowel sound in the word and tell whether it is a long or short vowel. Then put a few fish in the pocket chart and let children practice "catching" them with the fishing pole. Finally, invite two or more children to play the game.

Extending the Game

- For additional reinforcement, have children complete the practice page.

- Program copies of the blank fish to give children practice with other skills, such as word families, or beginning and ending sounds.

- Invite children to program their own fish to use in the game. They can draw pictures on the fish, or glue on pictures cut from magazines.

✷ HELPFUL TIPS

- ✷ If possible, use the toy magnetic fishing pole that comes with a magnetic fishing set (available at toy or department stores).

- ✷ Use copies of the blank fish on page 33 to create your own short and long vowel fish to use in the game.

- ✷ Invite children to trade in their fish from the game for fish-shaped crackers.

Short & Long Vowels

Fishing for Vowels

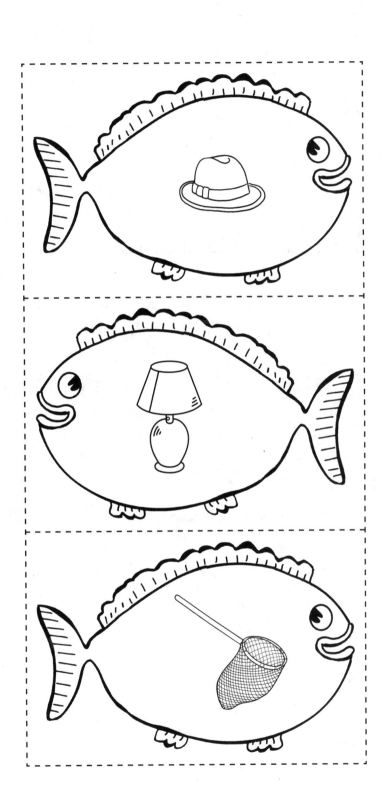

Players: 2 or more

Fishing for Vowels
Directions for Play

1 Use the fishing rod to catch a fish.

2 Take the fish off the line. Name the picture.

3 Does the word have a long vowel or a short vowel?
Check your answer on the back of the fish.
- If correct, keep the fish.
- If not, put the fish back.

4 Keep taking turns until all of the fish have been caught.
The player with the most fish wins the game.

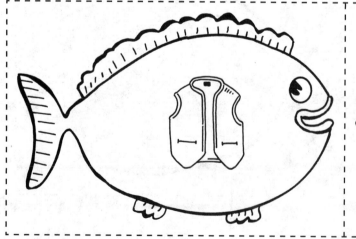 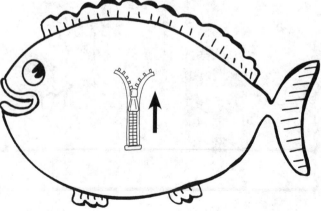

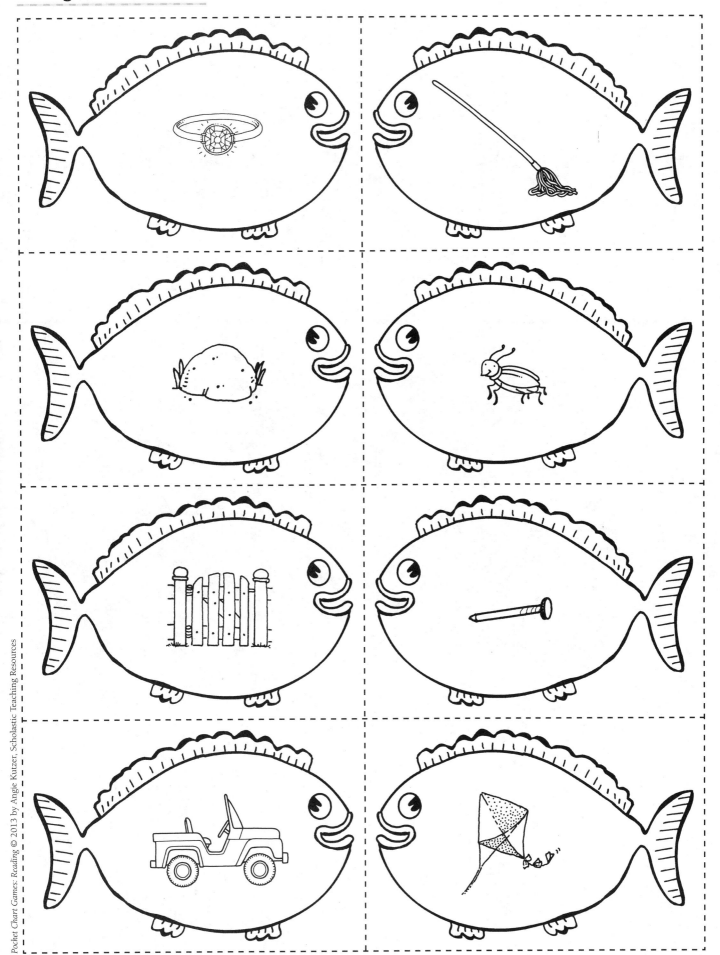

Name _____ Date _____

Vowel Swimmers

Say each word. What vowel sound is in it?
If it has a short vowel, color the fish yellow.
If it has a long vowel, color the fish red.

dog · slide · sled · seed · wig · cape · sun · flag · note · flute · clock · soap

Blends Picnic

Children identify blends as they move their ants from one end of the game board to the other.

Players: 2

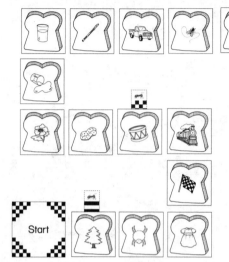
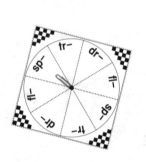

Materials

- title card (page 39)
- game directions (page 40)
- Start and Finish cards (page 39)
- picture cards (pages 39, 40, and 41)
- game spinner (page 42)
- game markers (page 42)
- answer key (page 42)
- large paper clip
- brass fastener
- pocket chart
- two clothespins

Getting Ready

Copy the title card, game directions, Start and Finish cards, picture cards, game spinner, game markers, and answer key. Color and cut out all of the game components. Place the title card in the top pocket of the pocket chart. Put the Start card in a pocket at the bottom left and the Finish card at the top right. Arrange the picture cards, facing out, in the pocket chart to create a path between the Start and Finish cards. Then use the paper clip and brass fastener to assemble the spinner. Use clothespins to clip the directions faceup to one side of the chart and the answer key facedown to the other side.

Introducing the Game

Show children each picture card and name it. Ask them to identify the consonant blend that begins the word. Or, display the picture cards, invite volunteers to spin the game spinner, and then identify a picture that begins with that blend. You might also work with the class to sort the cards by their beginning consonant blends. Finally, invite two children at a time to play the game.

Extending the Game

- Create more cards for different beginning consonant blends to use in the game. You can add those blends to the spinner by masking the printed blends and replacing them with the new blends.

- Place the spinner and picture cards in a learning center. Have children spin the spinner, find a corresponding card, then write the word on paper. Later, they can group their words by beginning blends.

HeLPFuL TiPS

- To add to the picnic theme of the game, spread out a picnic tablecloth and lay the pocket-chart game board on top of the tablecloth.

- To prepare the game for three or four players, copy additional game markers and color each one a different color. Or, use colored counters, paper squares, or foam shapes as game markers.

Consonant Blends

Blends Picnic

Pocket Chart Games: Reading © 2013 by Angie Kutzer, Scholastic Teaching Resources

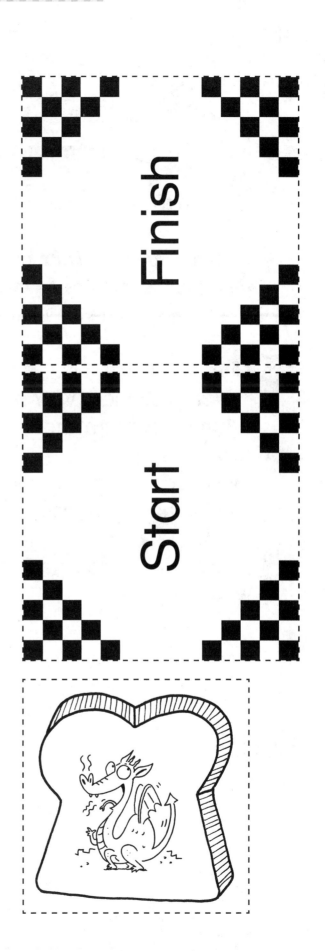

Finish

Start

Blends Picnic

Directions for Play

1 Choose a game marker. Place it on Start.

2 Spin the spinner. What blend did it land on?
Find the first picture on the path that begins with
that blend. Name the picture.

3 Check your answer.
   • If correct, move your marker to that space.
   • If not, your turn ends.

4 Move forward on each turn. Look for the closest
picture that begins with the blend on the spinner.

5 Keep taking turns. The first player to reach Finish
wins the game.

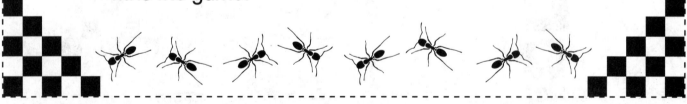

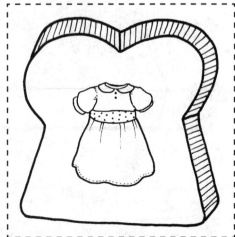

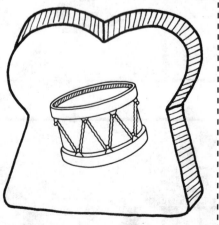

Pocket Chart Games: Reading © 2013 by Angie Kutzer, Scholastic Teaching Resources

Blends Picnic · Picture Cards

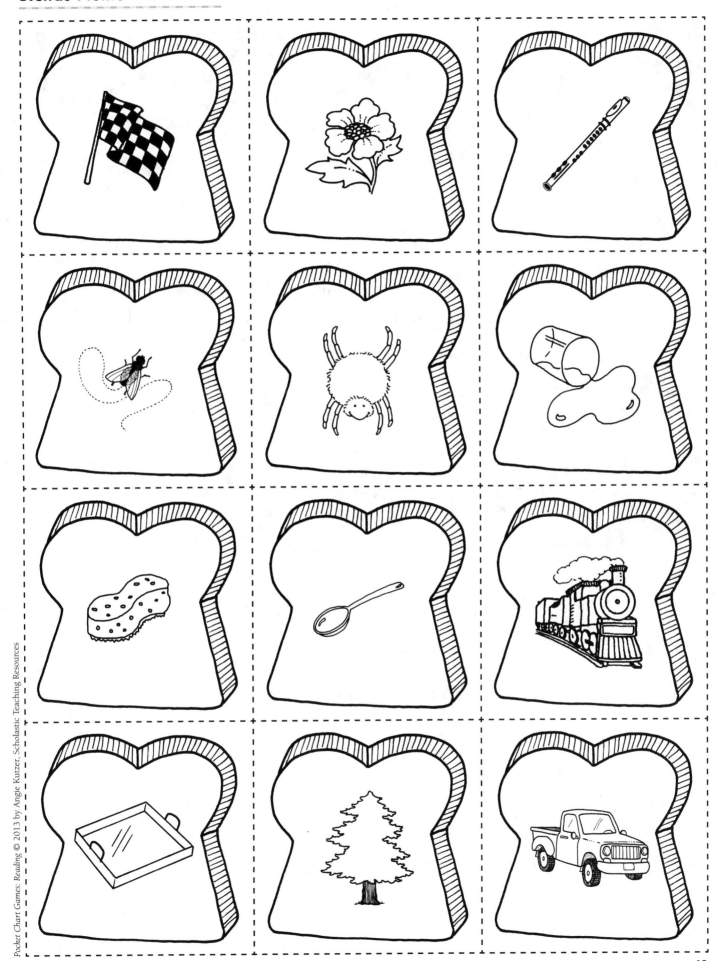

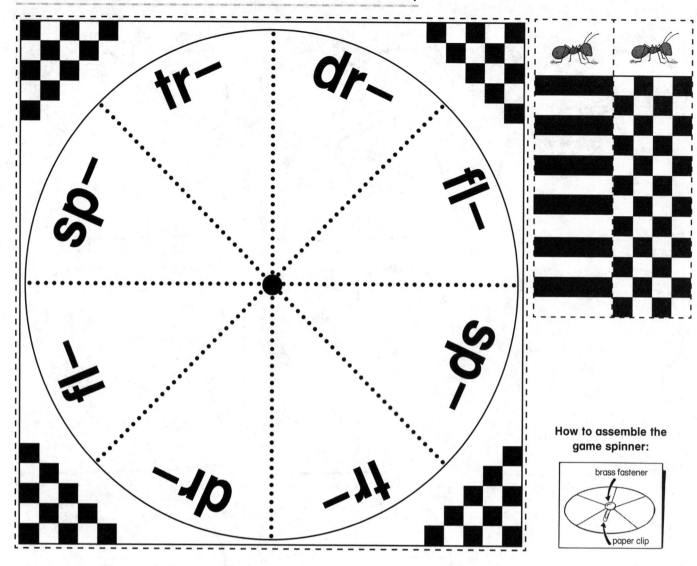

How to assemble the game spinner:

brass fastener

paper clip

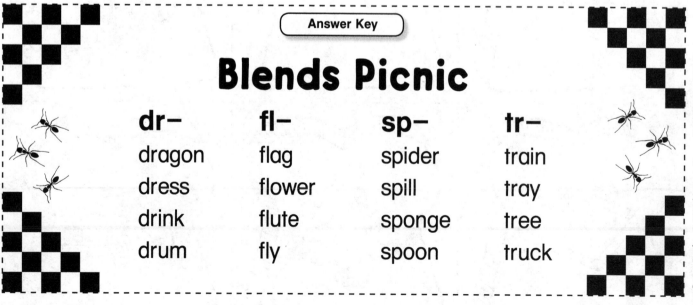

Answer Key

Blends Picnic

dr–	fl–	sp–	tr–
dragon	flag	spider	train
dress	flower	spill	tray
drink	flute	sponge	tree
drum	fly	spoon	truck

Pocket Chart Games: Reading © 2013 by Angie Kutzer, Scholastic Teaching Resources

Out of Sight!

Children read sight words as they to try to uncover the hidden aliens.

Players: 2 or more

Materials

* title card (page 44)
* game directions (page 45)
* Start and Finish cards (page 44)
* spaceships (page 46)
* aliens (pages 45 and 46)
* marker
* pocket chart
* sticky flags (one per player)
* clothespin
* coin

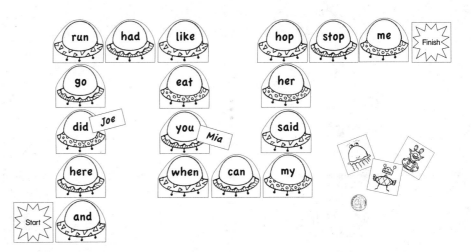

Getting Ready

Copy the title card, game directions, Start and Finish cards, spaceships, and aliens. Make six additional sets of the spaceships. Color and cut out all of the game components. (You should have 21 spaceships.) Place the title card in the top pocket of the pocket chart. Put the Start card in a pocket at the bottom left and the Finish card at the top right. Arrange the spaceships, facing out, in the pocket chart to create a winding path between Start and Finish. Finally, hide each alien behind a different spaceship. Use a clothespin to clip the directions faceup to one side of the chart.

Introducing the Game

Review the sight words on the spaceships with children. Then place the spaceships faceup in the chart, turn off the lights, and use a flashlight or laser pointer to point out the words in random order. Invite children to name each word in unison. Finally, invite two or more children to play the game.

Extending the Game

* Distribute spaceships for children to label with different sight words. Use them on your word wall. Then refer children to the word wall when completing their writing assignments.

* Label spaceships with letters and use for letter-recognition activities with younger students.

* Write space-themed vocabulary words on the spaceships and display on a word wall or learning center. Ask children to use the words in their research and for creative writing assignments.

HeLPFuL TiPS

* For additional rounds of play, hide the aliens behind different spaceships.

* If desired, double the number of aliens used in the game to give children more opportunities to find them.

Sight Words

Out of Sight!

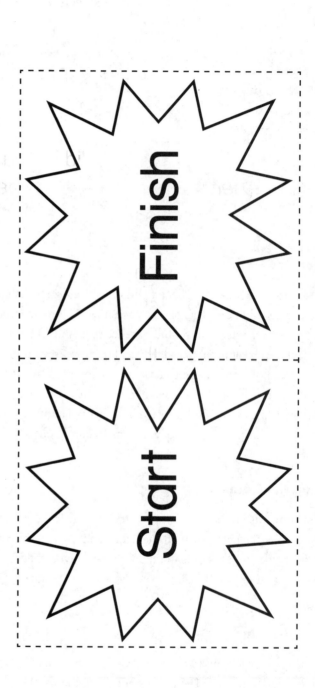

Finish

Start

Pocket Chart Games: Reading © 2013 by Angie Kutzer, Scholastic Teaching Resources

Players: 2 or more

Out of Sight!
Directions for Play

1 Write your name on a sticky flag.
Place your flag on Start.

2 Toss the coin. What did it land on?
- If *heads*, move your flag ahead one space.
- If *tails*, move two spaces.

3 What word is on the spaceship you landed on?
Read it aloud.

4 Did you read the word correctly? Ask other players.
- If so, look behind the spaceship.
- Is an alien there? If so, take the alien and keep it.

5 Keep taking turns until each player reaches Finish. The
player with the most aliens at the end of the game wins.

Pocket Chart Games: Reading © 2013 by Angie Kutzer, Scholastic Teaching Resources

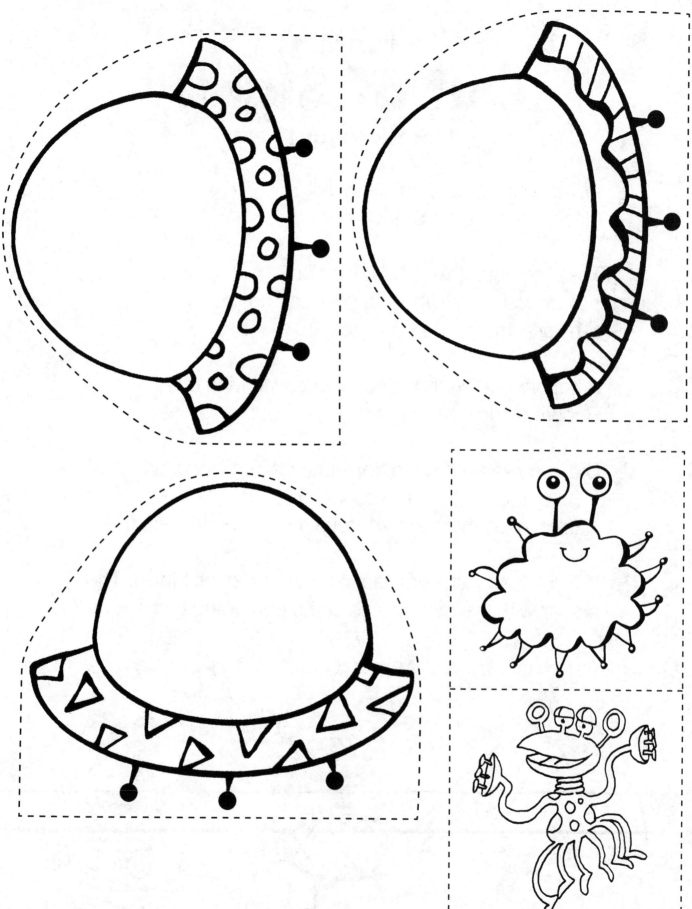

Word Family Camp

Children use letters and spelling patterns to create words with these word family tents.

Players: 2–4

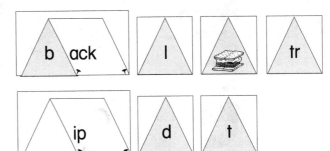

Materials

- title card (page 48)
- game directions (page 49)
- word family tents (pages 48 and 51)
- tent door cards (pages 49 and 50)
- answer key (page 51)
- pocket chart

Getting Ready

Copy the title card, game directions, word family tents, tent door cards, and answer key. Color and cut out all of the game components. Then cut out the triangle on each tent, where indicated. Place the title card in the top pocket of the pocket chart. Put a tent in each of the next four pockets, placing each one on the left side of the row. Shuffle the door cards and insert them facedown in the chart below the tents. Place the directions faceup and the answer key facedown in the bottom pocket. (Or use clothespins to clip them to the side of the chart.)

Introducing the Game

Display the word family tents along the chalk tray of your chalkboard. Sound out the word family ending on each tent. Then show children a door card with a letter. Name the letter and place the card behind one of the tent doors with the letter visible. Ask children to tell whether that letter makes a word with the word family ending on the tent. If so, write the word on the board above that tent. Repeat with different letters and alternating the tents. Afterward, invite 2–4 children at a time to play the game.

Extending the Game

- Put the tents and door cards in a learning center and have children use them as an independent activity. Ask them to write the words they make for each tent.

- After playing the game, reward children with a classroom snack of S'mores.

HeLPFuL TiPS

- You might copy each tent on a different color of paper.

- Create more word family tents and door cards so more players can play the game. Or, have children pair up with partners to play the game.

- Remind children that not all letters on the tent doors will make a word with the word family ending on a tent. For example, *y* and *ot* do not make a word (*yot*).

Word Families

Word Family Camp

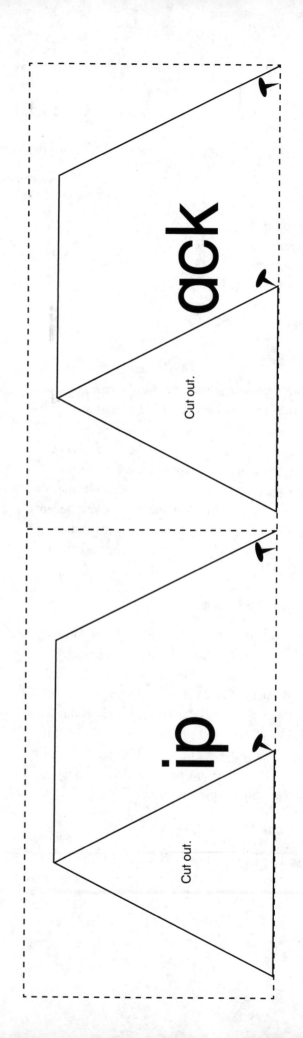

ack

Cut out.

ip

Cut out.

Pocket Chart Games: Reading © 2013 by Angie Kutzer, Scholastic Teaching Resources

Word Family Camp
Directions for Play

1 Choose a tent.

2 Take a door card. Did you pick a letter? If so, put it behind the opening of your tent. Does it make a word with the word family ending on your tent?

3 Check your answer.
- If correct, put the letter in the pocket to the right side of your tent.
- If not, put the letter back.

4 Did you pick a S'more? If so, you found a "free" card! Put it on the right side of your tent. Take another turn.

5 Keep taking turns. If you pick a letter you have already used, put it back. The first player to place five cards next to his or her tent wins the game.

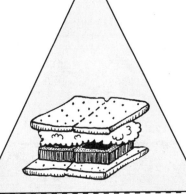
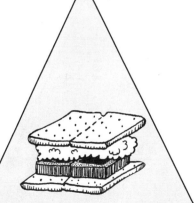

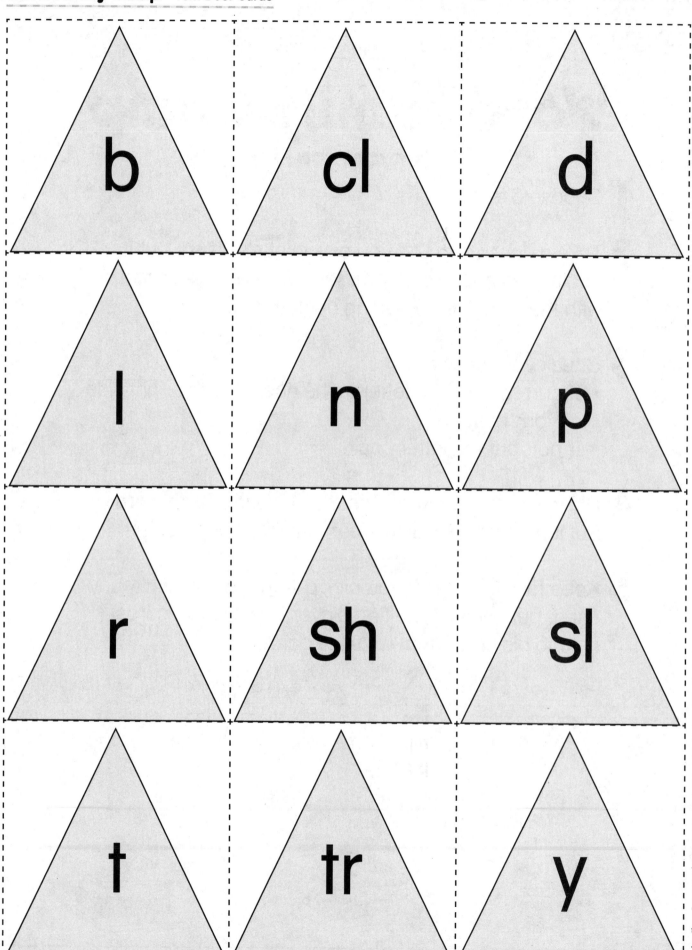

b

cl

d

l

n

p

r

sh

sl

t

tr

y

Pocket Chart Games: Reading © 2013 by Angie Kutzer, Scholastic Teaching Resources

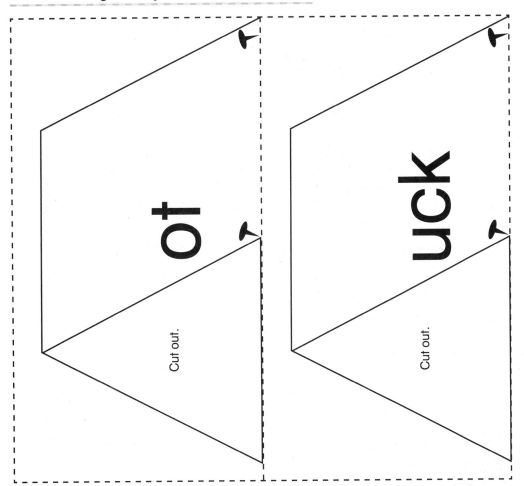

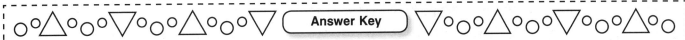

Word Family Camp

ack	**ip**	**ot**	**uck**
back	**cl**ip	**cl**ot	**b**uck
clack	**d**ip	**d**ot	**cl**uck
lack	**l**ip	**l**ot	**d**uck
pack	**n**ip	**n**ot	**l**uck
rack	**p**ip	**p**ot	**p**uck
shack	**r**ip	**r**ot	**sh**uck
slack	**sh**ip	**sh**ot	**t**uck
tack	**sl**ip	**sl**ot	**tr**uck
track	**t**ip	**t**ot	**y**uck
yack	**tr**ip	**tr**ot	
	yip		

Pocket Chart Games: Reading © 2013 by Angie Kutzer, Scholastic Teaching Resources

Syllable Sea

Children count the syllables in the names of sea animals.

Players: 2

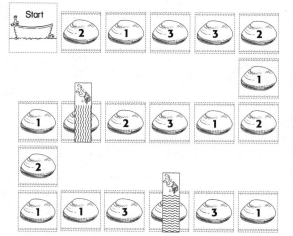

Materials

- title card (page 53)
- game directions (page 54)
- Start and Finish cards (page 53)
- sea animal cards (pages 54 and 55)
- shell cards (page 56)
- game markers (page 53)
- answer key (page 56)
- pocket chart
- small paper bag
- two clothespins
- practice page (page 57)

Getting Ready

Copy the title card, game directions, Start and Finish cards, sea animal and shell cards, game markers, and answer key. Make six additional sets of the shell cards. Color and cut out all of the game components. (You should have 21 shell cards.) Place the title card in the top pocket of the pocket chart. Then put the Start card on the left in the pocket below the title. Place the Finish card in the bottom pocket on the right. Shuffle the shell cards and use them to create a curvy path between Start and Finish. Put the sea animal cards in the paper bag. Use clothespins to clip the directions faceup to one side of the chart and the answer key facedown to the other side.

Introducing the Game

Show each sea animal card to children and name it. Ask children to tell how many syllables are in the word. Encourage them to say the word slowly and clap out the syllables, counting as they go. Write the syllable count on the board. Finally, invite two children at a time to play the game.

Extending the Game

- For additional reinforcement, have children complete the practice page.
- Put the sea animal cards in a learning center, and have children sort them by syllable count.
- Provide letter cards with the animal cards. Have children match the letter to the beginning sound of each animal. You might also have them listen for and match sounds at the end of the animal names.

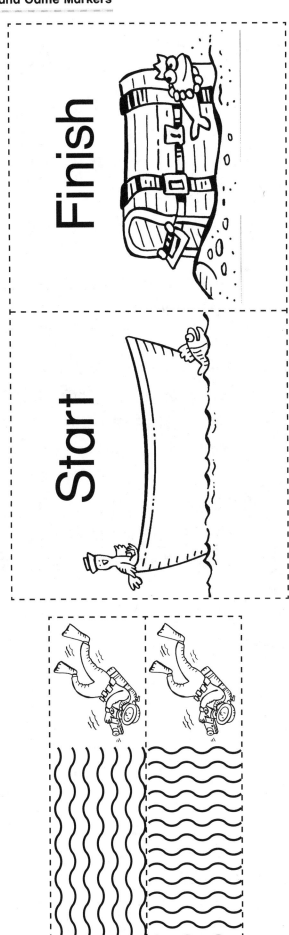

Players: 2

Syllable Sea
Directions for Play

1 Choose a game marker. Place it on Start.

2 Take a card out of the bag. Name the animal. How many syllables are in that word?

3 Check your answer.
- If correct, move your marker to the next shell with that number.
- If not, your turn ends.

4 Keep taking turns. Put your card back in the bag after each turn. The first player to reach Finish wins the game.

eel

crab

seal

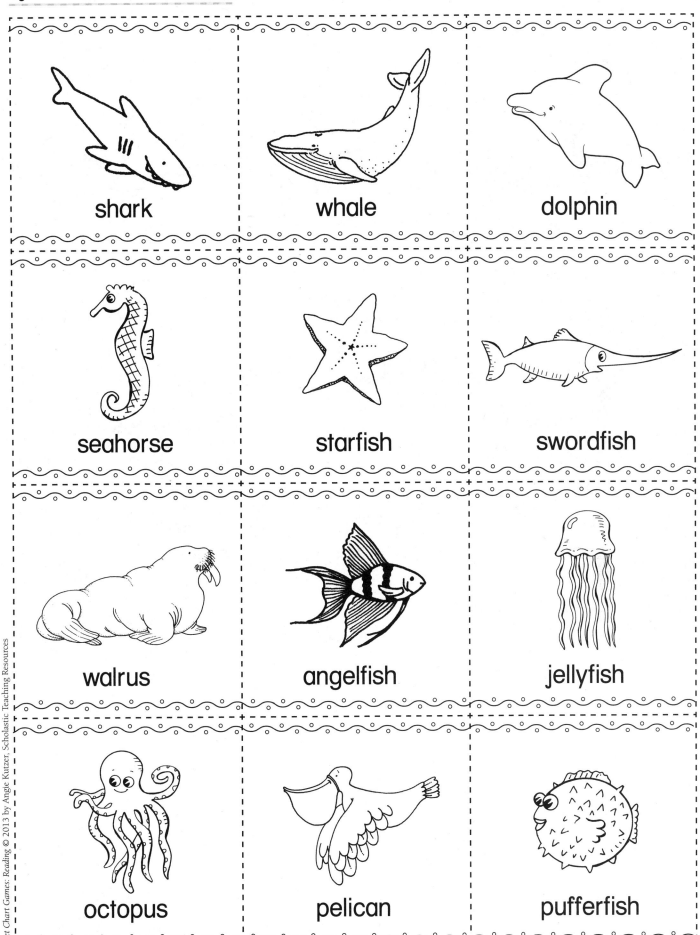

shark

whale

dolphin

seahorse

starfish

swordfish

walrus

angelfish

jellyfish

octopus

pelican

pufferfish

Syllable Sea

1 syllable	2 syllables	3 syllables
crab	dolphin	angelfish
eel	seahorse	jellyfish
seal	starfish	octopus
shark	swordfish	pelican
whale	walrus	pufferfish

Pocket Chart Games: Reading © 2013 by Angie Kutzer, Scholastic Teaching Resources

Syllables at the Seashore

Name each picture.
How many syllables does the word have?
Write that number in the box.

1. ☐ seashell

2. ☐ umbrella

3. ☐ hat

4. ☐ float

5. ☐ towel

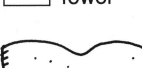

6. ☐ sunglasses

7. ☐ seagull

8. ☐ kite

9. ☐ bucket

Word Connections

Children find the word pairs that are used to make compound words.

Players: 2

Materials

- title card (page 59)
- game directions (page 60)
- picture cards (page 59)
- word cards (page 61)
- answer key (page 60)
- pocket chart

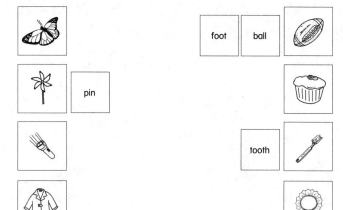

Getting Ready

Copy the title card, game directions, picture and word cards, and answer key. Color and cut out all of the game components. Place the title card in the top pocket of the pocket chart. Place each of four picture cards in a different row on the left side of the chart. Place the other four picture cards in the same rows on the right side. Shuffle the word cards and insert them facedown in the chart below the picture cards. Place the directions faceup and the answer key facedown in the bottom pocket. (Or use a clothespin to clip the answers to the side of the chart.)

Introducing the Game

Explain to children that a compound word is made up of two small words that have been put together. Display each picture card and have children name it. Ask them to tell which two small words make up the compound word. Then write those words on the board, or show children the corresponding word cards. Finally, invite two children at a time to play the game.

Extending the Game

- Put the picture and word cards in a learning center for children to use as an independent matching activity.

- Invite children to cut out pictures from magazines to make additional picture cards to use for the game.

- Have children write sentences using the compound words from the game.

✴ HeLPFuL TiPS ✴

- ✴ For younger children, you might copy the first word of each compound word on one color of paper and the second word on a different color.

- ✴ Make additional picture and word cards to give children practice with other compound words.

Compound Words

Word Connections

Players: 2

Word Connections
Directions for Play

1 Choose four picture cards on one side of the chart.

2 Take a word card and read it.

3 Can the word be used to make one of your compound words? Check your answer.
  • If correct, put the card next to that compound word.
  • If not, put the card back.

4 Keep taking turns. The first player to find all of the words that match his or her compound words wins the game.

Answer Key

Word Connections

butterfly

flashlight

pinwheel

sunflower

cupcake

football

raincoat

toothbrush

Pocket Chart Games: Reading © 2013 by Angie Kutzer, Scholastic Teaching Resources

flash	ball	rain	flower
light	pin	coat	tooth
foot	wheel	sun	brush
butter	fly	cup	cake

Buggy Contractions

Children find the words on ladybug cards that make up different contractions.

Players: 2 or more

Materials

- title card (page 63)
- game directions (page 64)
- grass strips (page 65)
- ladybug cards (pages 63, 65, and 66)
- answer key (page 64)
- pocket chart

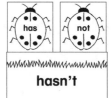

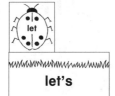
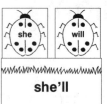

Getting Ready

Copy the title card, game directions, grass strips, ladybug cards, and answer key. Color and cut out all of the game components. Place the title card in the top pocket of the pocket chart. Place each of four grass strips in a different row on the left side of the chart. Place the other four strips in the same rows on the right side. Shuffle the ladybug cards and insert them facedown in the chart below the grass strips. Place the directions faceup and the answer key facedown in the bottom pocket. (Or use a clothespin to clip the answers to the side of the chart.)

Introducing the Game

Explain to children that a contraction is made up of two words. Tell them that the apostrophe stands for letters that have been removed when putting the words together to make the contraction. Then display each grass strip and have children read the contraction. Ask them to tell which two words are used to make up the contraction. Write those words on the board, or show children the corresponding ladybug cards. Then have children tell which letters were removed. Afterward, invite two children at a time to play the game.

Extending the Game

- Place the grass strips and ladybug cards in a learning center for children to use as a matching activity.
- Have children write sentences using the contractions on the grass strips.

✦ HeLPFuL TiPs ✦

- ✻ You might copy the ladybugs labeled with the first word of each contraction on one color of paper and the ladybugs with the second word on a different color.
- ✻ Make additional grass strips and ladybug cards to give children practice with other contractions.

Contractions

Buggy Contractions

Pocket Chart Games: Reading © 2013 by Angie Kutzer, Scholastic Teaching Resources

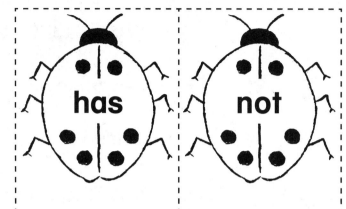

has   not

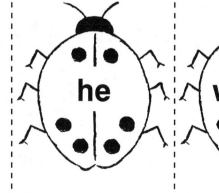

he   would

Players: 2 or more

Buggy Contractions
Directions for Play

1 Choose four grass strips on one side of the chart.

2 Take a ladybug. Read the word.

3 Can the word be used to make one of your contractions? Check your answer.
  • If correct, put the ladybug above that grass strip.
  • If not, put the ladybug back.

4 Keep taking turns. The first player to find the ladybug words for all of his or her grass strips wins the game.

Answer Key

Buggy Contractions

hasn't	has not
he'd	he would
I'm	I am
it's	it is
let's	let us
she'll	she will
we've	we have
you're	you are

Pocket Chart Games: Reading © 2013 by Angie Kutzer, Scholastic Teaching Resources

he'd

it's

she'll

you're

hasn't

I'm

let's

we've

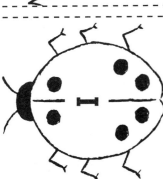

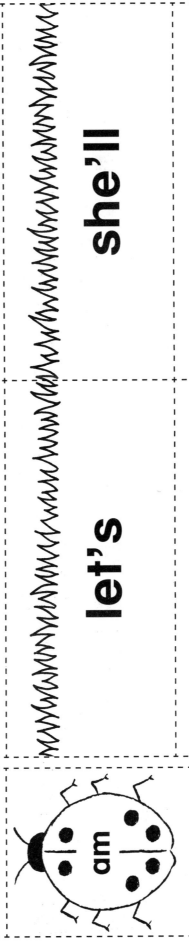

Pocket Chart Games: Reading © 2013 by Angie Kutzer, Scholastic Teaching Resources

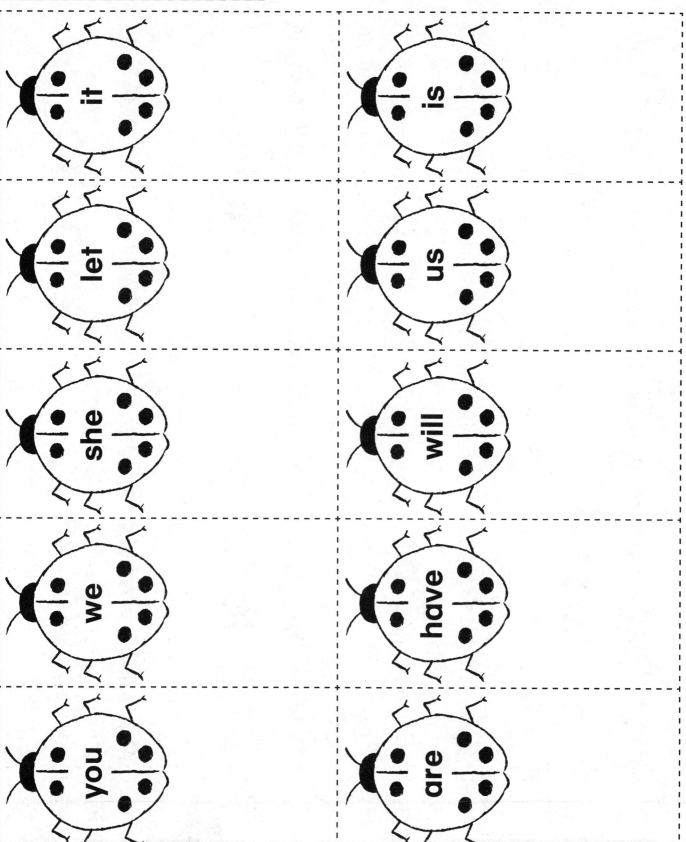

Doghouse Opposites

Children read words and identify their antonyms as they move the dog toward their team's doghouse.

Players: 2 teams

Materials

- title card (page 68)
- game directions (page 69)
- dog and team cards (page 68)
- paws (page 72)
- bone cards (pages 69, 70, and 71)
- game spinner (page 70)
- answer key (page 71)
- large paper clip
- brass fastener
- pocket chart

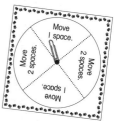

Getting Ready

Copy the title card, game directions, dog, team cards, paws, bone cards, game spinner, and answer key. Color and cut out all of the game components. Use the paper clip and brass fastener to assemble the spinner. Then place the title card in the top pocket of the pocket chart. Put a team card at each end of a row below the title. Insert the paws between the team cards, spacing them evenly across the row. Next, place the dog in front of the middle paw. Shuffle the bone cards and put them facedown in the chart below the row of paws. Place the directions faceup and the answer key facedown in the bottom pocket. (Or use a clothespin to clip the answers to the side of the chart.)

Introducing the Game

Read the word on each bone card. Ask children to name the antonym for the word. Then have them brainstorm other opposite pairs. Finally, form teams of 3–4 children and invite two teams at a time to play the game.

Extending the Game

- Label copies of the blank card with antonyms of the words on the other bone cards. Place the bones in a learning center for children to use as a matching activity.
- Make a set of bones labeled with synonym pairs for children to match.
- Create a set of bone cards labeled with letters to give younger children practice in letter recognition.

HeLPFuL TiP

- For a shorter game, have the teams take a specific number of turns. Then determine the winner by identifying which team's doghouse the dog is closest to.

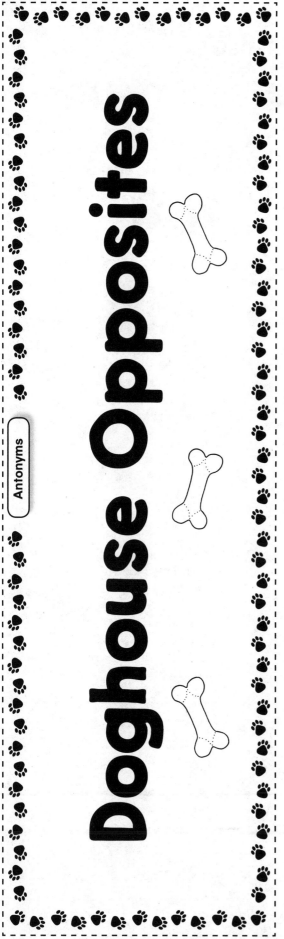

Antonyms

Doghouse Opposites

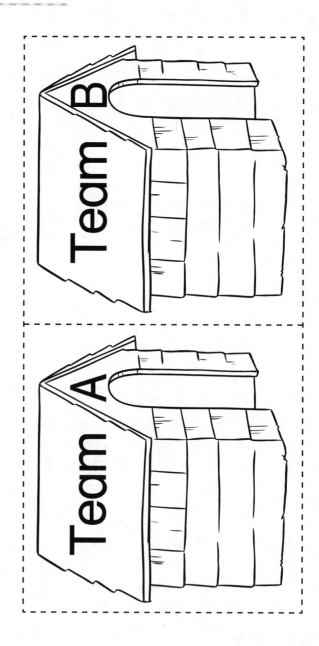

Team B

Team A

Pocket Chart Games: Reading © 2013 by Angie Kutzer, Scholastic Teaching Resources

Players: 2 teams

Doghouse Opposites
Directions for Play

1 Each team chooses a team card. The first player on Team A goes first.

2 Take out a bone card. Read the word.

3 What is the opposite of your word? Check your answer.

4 If correct, spin the spinner. What did it land on? Move the dog that many paws toward your team's doghouse. Put the bone back in the pocket.

5 Teams A and B keep taking turns moving the dog back and forth. The first team to move the dog to its team card—on an exact count—is the winner.

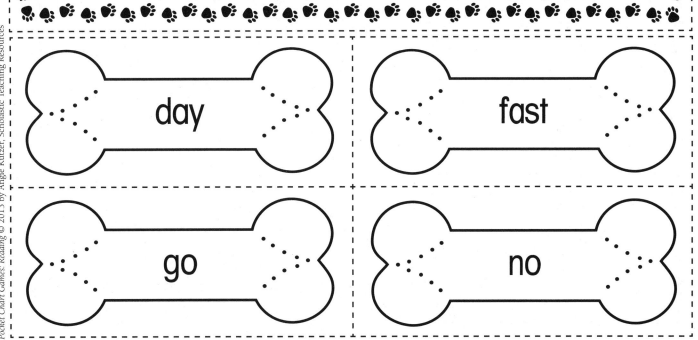

day

fast

go

no

Pocket Chart Games: Reading © 2013 by Angie Kutzer, Scholastic Teaching Resources

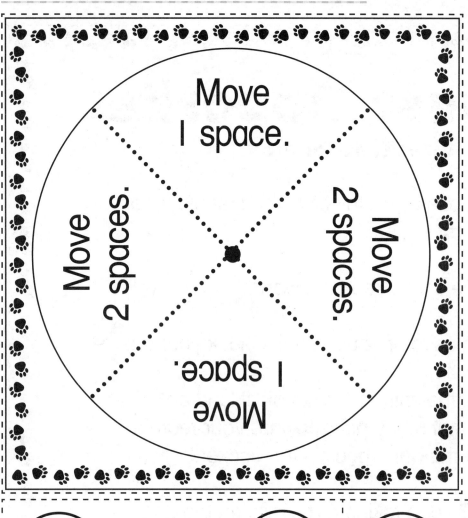

How to assemble the game spinner:

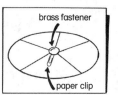

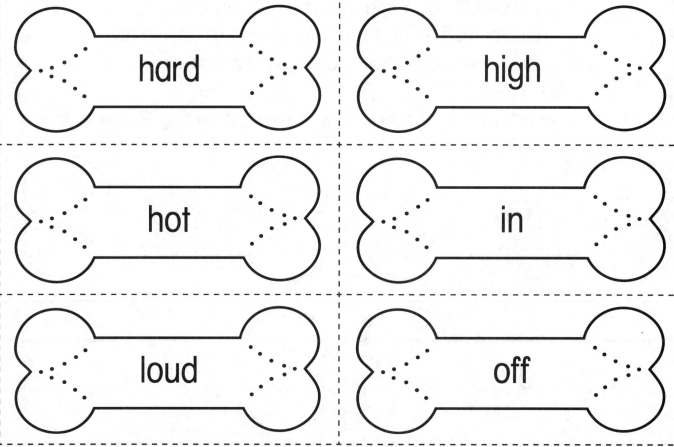

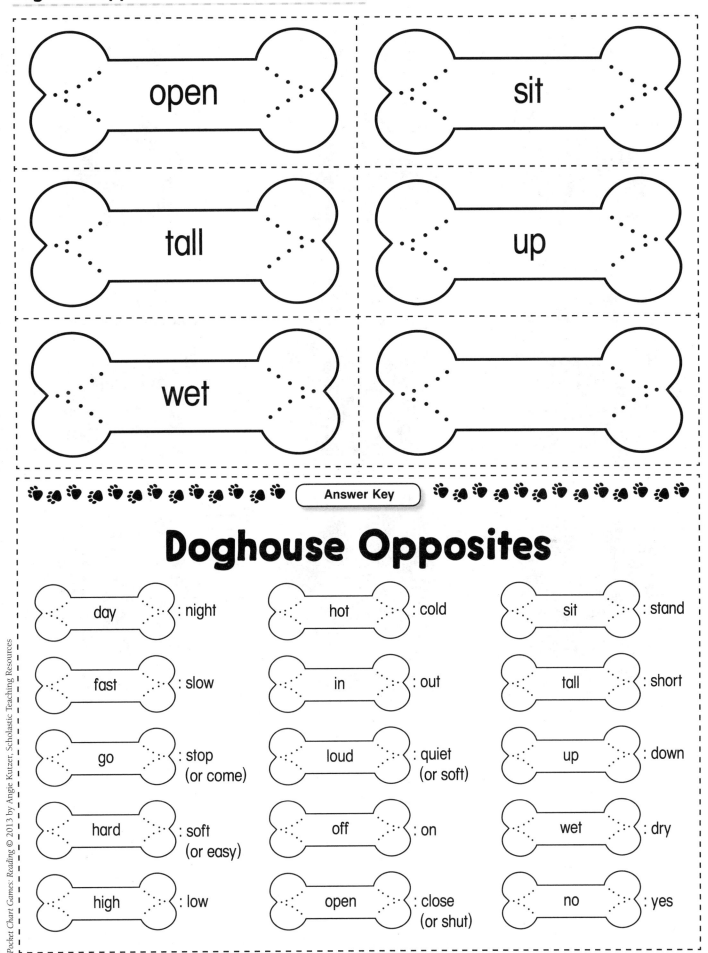

open

sit

tall

up

wet

Answer Key

Doghouse Opposites

day : night	hot : cold	sit : stand
fast : slow	in : out	tall : short
go : stop (or come)	loud : quiet (or soft)	up : down
hard : soft (or easy)	off : on	wet : dry
high : low	open : close (or shut)	no : yes

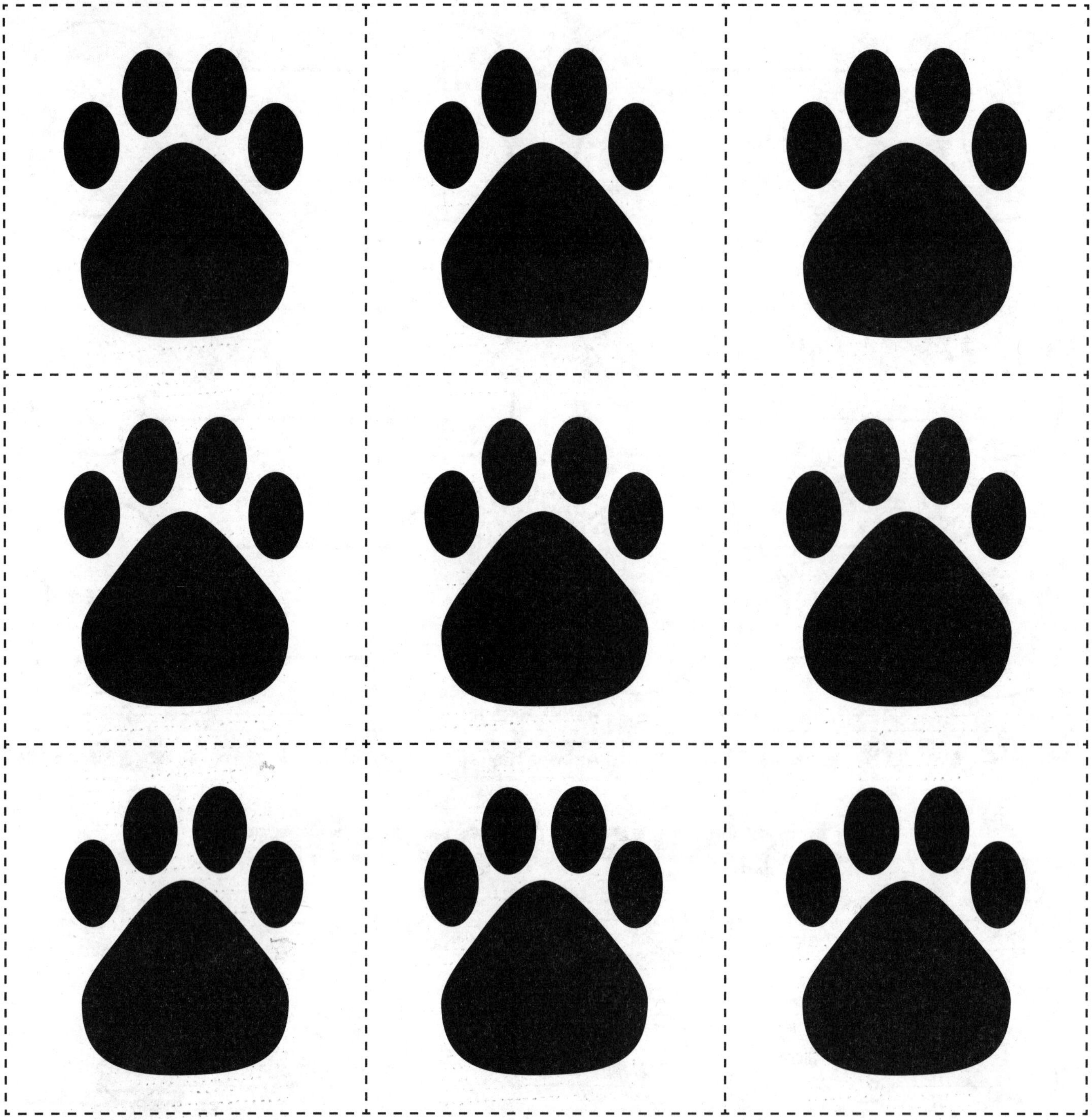

Banana Climb

Children identify nouns and verbs in a race to move their monkey to the banana.

Players: 2

Materials

- title card (page 74)
- game directions (page 75)
- monkeys and banana cards (page 74)
- word cards (page 76)
- answer key (page 75)
- pocket chart
- small paper bag

Getting Ready

Copy the title card, game directions, monkeys, banana cards, word cards, and answer key. Color and cut out all of the game components. Place the title card in the top pocket of the pocket chart. Put the banana cards in the pocket below the title, placing one to the left of the title and the other to the right. Insert a monkey card in the bottom pocket directly below each banana card. (Leave five or more empty pockets between the two cards.) Then put the word cards in the bag. Place the directions faceup and the answer key facedown in a pocket at the bottom of the chart. (Or use clothespins to clip them to the side of the chart.)

Introducing the Game

Explain to children that nouns are naming words and verbs are action words. Show each word card to children. Have them read the card and tell whether the word is a noun or verb. Then invite children to brainstorm other nouns and verbs related to a zoo and zoo animals. Finally, invite two children at a time to play the game.

Extending the Game

- For a variation, assign each player one part of speech: noun or verb. Each time the player draws a card for the assigned part of speech, he or she moves his or her monkey up one row.

- Place the word cards in a learning center for children to use as an independent sorting activity.

HELPFUL TIPS

- If desired, place brown squares in each pocket between the banana and monkey cards to create a vertical path for the monkey to "climb."

- To prepare the game for up to four players, copy two more monkey and banana cards and make additional word cards.

Pocket Chart Games: Reading © 2013 by Angie Kutzer, Scholastic Teaching Resources

Nouns & Verbs

Banana Climb

Banana Climb

Directions for Play

1 Choose a monkey.

2 Take a card from the bag. Read the word.

3 Is the word a noun or a verb?
Check your answer.

4 Is your answer correct?
- If so, move your monkey up one row, if your word is a noun.
- Move your monkey up two rows if it is a verb.

5 Keep taking turns. Put your card back in the bag after each turn. The first player to reach his or her bananas at the top—on an exact count—wins the game.

Answer Key

Banana Climb

Nouns		Verbs	
cat	grass	crawl	run
feet	lion	eat	sit
food	snake	hop	spin
gate	tree	jump	stomp

Pocket Chart Games: Reading © 2013 by Angie Kutzer, Scholastic Teaching Resources

cat	grass	crawl	run
feet	lion	eat	sit
food	snake	hop	spin
gate	tree	jump	stomp

Pocket Chart Games: Reading © 2013 by Angie Kutzer, Scholastic Teaching Resources

Describe It!

Children match adjectives to the pictures they describe.

Players: 2–3

Materials

- title card (page 78)
- game directions (page 79)
- picture cards (pages 78 and 80)
- word cards (page 80)
- answer key (page 79)
- pocket chart

Getting Ready

Copy the title card, game directions, picture and word cards, and answer key. Color and cut out all of the game components. Place the title card in the top pocket of the pocket chart. Shuffle all of the cards. Then arrange the cards facedown in the pocket chart to make a 4-by-4 grid. Place the directions faceup and the answer key facedown in a pocket at the bottom of the chart. (Or use a clothespin to clip the answers to the side of the chart.)

Introducing the Game

Show children each game card. Ask them to name the picture or read the word. Then display the picture cards in an array. Read one word card at a time and have children identify the picture it describes. Invite a volunteer to remove that card and pair it up with the word card. Afterward, invite two or three children at a time to play the game.

Extending the Game

- Create additional cards to use in the game. You might use 10 or 12 pairs of cards in the game for more advanced children.
- Put the game cards in a learning center for children to use as an independent matching activity.
- Display the picture and word cards together, then have children write sentences using the noun and adjective pairs.

HELPFUL TIPS

- To add color and interest to the game, glue decorative wrapping paper to the back of the cards and trim to fit.
- Show children how to arrange the cards in a grid pattern so they can set up the game for additional rounds of play.

Adjectives

Describe It!

<Players: 2–3>

Describe It!
Directions for Play

1 The first player takes two cards.

2 Did you pick a picture and a word card?
- If not, put the cards back.
- If so, name the picture and read the word.

3 Does the word describe the picture?
Check your answer.
- If so, keep the cards.
- If not, put the cards back.

4 Keep taking turns. The game ends when all the cards have been used. The player with the most cards wins the game.

< Answer Key >

Describe It!

cold: furry: wet:

crunchy: hot: windy:

fast: silly:

| cold | hot |

| crunchy | silly |

| fast | wet |

| furry | windy |

Pocket Chart Games: Reading © 2013 by Angie Kutzer, Scholastic Teaching Resources